D0185703

I Know Someone Who Is
Obese

Sue Barraclough

www.raintreepublishers.co.uk
Visit our website to find out
more information about
Raintree books.

To order:

☎ Phone 0845 6044371

▤ Fax +44 (0) 1865 312263

▧ Email myorders@raintreepublishers.co.uk

Customers from outside the UK please telephone +44 1865 312262

Raintree is an imprint of Capstone Global Library
Limited, a company incorporated in England and
Wales having its registered office at 7 Pilgrim Street,
London, EC4V 6LB – Registered company number:
6695582

Text © Capstone Global Library Limited 2011
First published in hardback in 2011
The moral rights of the proprietor have been asserted.

Edited by Rebecca Rissman, Dan Nunn,
   and Catherine Veitch
Designed by Steve Mead and Joanna Hinton Malivoire
Picture research by Tracy Cummins
Originated by Capstone Global Library
Printed and bound in China by Leo Paper Products Ltd

ISBN 978 1 406 22084 1
15 14 13 12 11
10 9 8 7 6 5 4 3 2 1

British Library Cataloguing in Publication Data
Barraclough, Sue.
I know someone who is obese. –
(Understanding health issues)
616.3'98-dc22
A full catalogue record for this book is available from
the British Library.

Acknowledgements
We would like to thank the following for permission
to reproduce photographs: Corbis pp. **4** (© Peter
Frank), **5** (© moodboard), **9** (© moodboard), **11** (©
Image Source), **17** (© Jose Luis Pelaez, Inc./Blend
Images), **23** (© Corbis); Getty Images pp. **8** (Justin
Sullivan), **12** (3660 Group Inc.), **18** (Justin Sullivan), **20**
(Jupiterimages), **21** (Annika Erickson), **22** (Jonatan
Fernstrom), **24** (Philip Lee Harvey), **25** (Stephan
Gladieu), **26** (Rick Diamond/WireImage), **27** (Holly
Farrell/ABC); Photo Researchers, Inc. pp. **6** (Pasieka), **13**
(Ian Hooton), **14** (Gusto), **15** (Gusto); Shutterstock pp.
10 (© Noam Armonn), **19** (© Newphotoservice), **29** (©
Monkey Business Images).

Cover photograph of a boy and his mother in a
pool reproduced with permission of Superstock
(© age fotostock).

We would like to thank Ashley Wolinski and Matthew
Siegel for their invaluable help in the preparation of
this book.

Every effort has been made to contact copyright
holders of any material reproduced in this book. Any
omissions will be rectified in subsequent printings if
notice is given to the publisher.

Contents

Some words are printed in bold, **like this**. You can find out what they mean in the glossary.

Do you know someone who is obese?

You may know someone who is obese. A child who is obese is much bigger than the other children in class. Someone who is obese may find it hard to play active games.

It is important for everyone to have good friends.

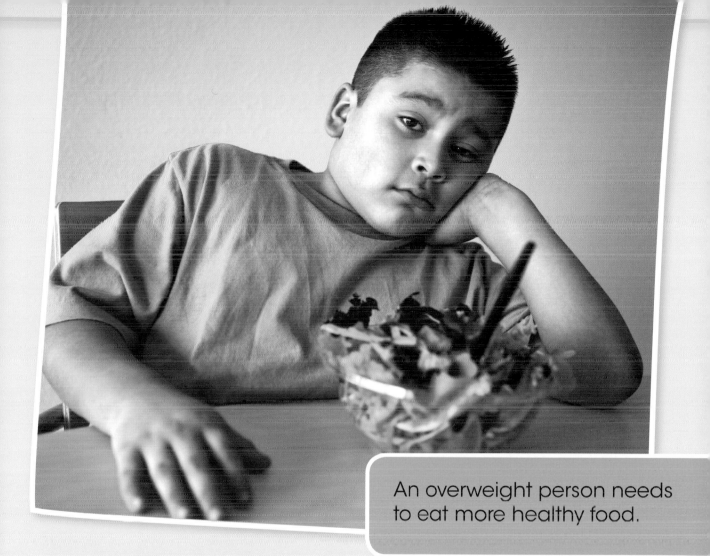

An overweight person needs to eat more healthy food.

A person who is obese may have to be careful about what they eat. Someone who is obese may often feel tired because they do not sleep well.

What does it mean to be obese?

Being obese means having too much **body fat**. A body uses food to give it **energy** to move and grow. A body keeps energy that it does not use as body fat. The fat is stored under the skin in special **cells**.

Fat cells can grow larger. They are what make bodies grow larger.

underweight	not enough body fat
healthy weight	the right amount of body fat
overweight	too much body fat
obese	so much body fat that it causes health problems

Each body is different so a healthy weight is different from person to person. Doctors do a test to find out if someone is obese rather than overweight. This test uses numbers from height and weight to work out if a person has a weight problem.

What causes obesity?

The main causes of obesity are eating too many sweet and fatty foods and not taking enough exercise. People put on weight when they eat more food than the body can use.

A doctor can help work out why a person is obese.

Obesity can be **genetic**, which means that it runs in a family. If your parents are obese there is a good chance you will be, too. However, unhealthy body shapes and weights are only partly due to genes.

Many children learn unhealthy eating **habits** from their parents.

Why are more people becoming obese?

Obesity is a growing problem in the world. In the last 30 years, more and more people have become obese. One reason is that we all eat too much unhealthy food.

Many foods do not contain **nutrients** that a body needs to stay healthy.

Lifts, escalators, and automatic doors make life easier but they also make us less active.

More people are obese now because of the way we live. We use more machines and gadgets to help us so we are less active. Driving cars means that we walk and cycle less.

Living with obesity

Someone who is obese may have heart problems.

Obesity can cause dangerous health problems. The heart of an obese person has to work harder and it may stop working well. Fat can block **arteries**, the tubes that carry blood around the body. This means they stop working well too.

People who are obese often develop **diabetes**. Diabetes is when there is too much sugar in the blood because the body cannot use it properly. Diabetes is treated with diet control and **insulin injections** or pills.

A person with diabetes has to take medication or have regular injections.

How does it feel?

People who are obese often get teased or bullied because of their weight. Someone who is obese may be called names, left out of games and activities, and sometimes finds it hard to make friends.

People who are obese sometimes eat because it makes them feel better.

An overweight person often does not feel like being active.

Someone who is overweight or obese is more likely to feel sad and lack **energy**.

An obese person may:
- have stiff joints
- have problems breathing
- have bad moods.

Healthy eating

One of the best ways to overcome obesity is to make small changes to eating **habits**. Try to:
- eat different healthy foods
- eat less by having smaller portions
- drink more water.

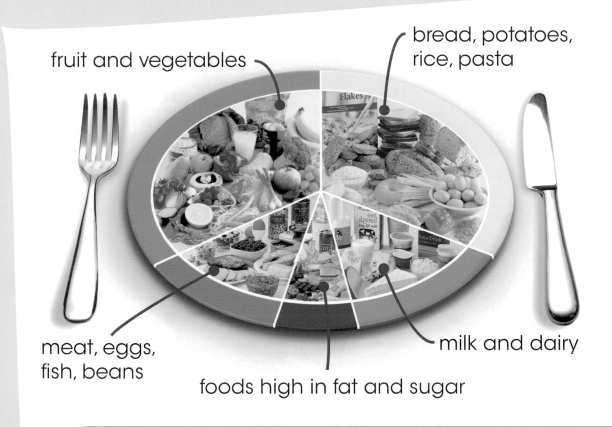

fruit and vegetables

bread, potatoes, rice, pasta

meat, eggs, fish, beans

foods high in fat and sugar

milk and dairy

Use the eatwell plate to help you choose which food to eat more of and which you should cut down on.

Taking part in food shopping is a good way to learn about healthy food.

Healthy eating habits include:
- having meals and healthy snacks at regular times
- not eating while watching television or doing homework
- stopping eating when you are full
- cooking and eating together as a family.

Keeping fit

Regular exercise builds strong bones and **muscles** and a healthy heart.

One of the best ways to stay healthy is to take plenty of exercise. This means you use up the **energy** in the food you eat so you have less **body fat**. To stay healthy, children need to try to do one hour of exercise every day.

It is important to work together to plan to be more active. Families and friends can plan to do more active things in the evenings or at weekends.

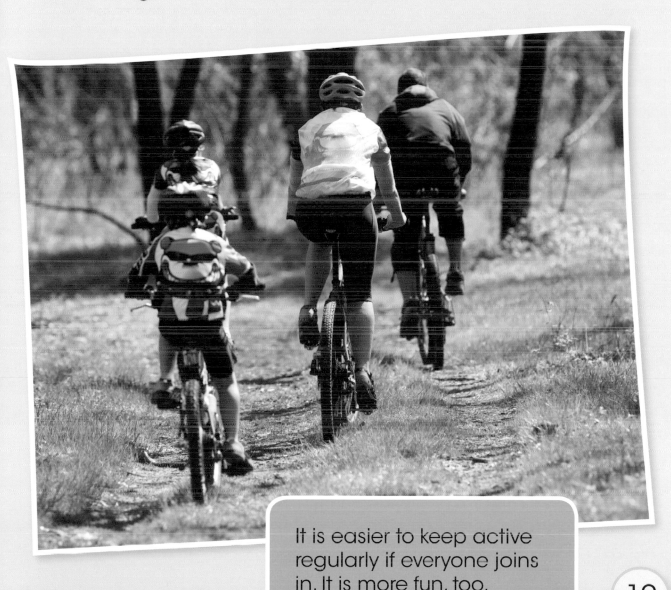

It is easier to keep active regularly if everyone joins in. It is more fun, too.

Being a friend

You can be a good friend to someone who is obese by eating healthy food and encouraging your friend to do the same. Everybody needs friends to help and support them.

Friends and family can work together to make better food choices.

Exercise can make you feel hot and sweaty but this usually means it is doing your body good.

You can help someone who is obese by:
- not nagging or teasing about exercise or food as this will make them feel worse
- helping with **self esteem** by noticing when your friend has done well
- planning to take small steps together to change unhealthy **habits**.

What can I do?

Someone who is obese may be teased because of their size. Sometimes friends, family, and even strangers can say hurtful things. You can support a friend by being with them, and helping them to ignore unkind remarks.

Good friends help and support each other.

You should also talk to an adult if you know someone who is bullied. You will be helping your friend.

If you are being teased or bullied you should tell a teacher or an adult. Nobody deserves to be treated unkindly.

How can I help?

You can help an obese friend by:

- doing more active things together after school such as walking the dog or bike riding
- doing fewer **inactive** things together such as watching television or playing video games
- planning activities for weekends that will keep you both fit.

Encourage your friends to play outdoors. This will help you all keep fit.

Taking part in sporting activities can make you feel confident about yourself.

You can help a friend who is obese by understanding that they might find some activities difficult. Be patient, try to do things at their speed, and help them do their best.

Famous people

Jennifer Hudson is a famous American singer and actress. Jennifer has lost weight because she changed her eating and exercise **habits**.

Jennifer has cut down on the amount of food she eats and exercises every day to stay healthy.

Chef Jamie Oliver has **campaigned** to get children eating more healthy food, particularly at school. Obesity is a problem for more and more children so it is important to try to do something about it.

Obesity – true or false?

Obesity runs in families. If your parents are obese then you will be too.

FALSE! Obesity can run in families but if you eat healthily and take plenty of exercise you can be fit and healthy.

Body fat is bad for you.

FALSE! We need some body fat to be healthy. It is only when we have too much body fat that it is unhealthy.

Some people can eat all sorts of unhealthy foods and not put on weight.

TRUE! Our bodies do use food at different rates. However, eating lots of unhealthy foods can cause health problems for everyone.

Glossary

arteries tubes that carry blood from the heart and around the body

body fat substance under the skin that helps to keep us warm

campaign take action to make something better

cells tiny living parts that fit together to make your body

diabetes condition in which the body cannot control the amount of sugar in the blood

energy something that makes things work, move, or change

genetic something that is controlled by genes. A gene is a part of a cell that is passed from parent to child. Genes control things such as body shape and hair colour.

habits things that we do everyday or very often

inactive not doing anything, such as watching television

injection people use an injection to take medicine into their bodies through a needle

insulin substance that the body uses to control the amount of sugar in the blood

muscles strong, stretchy body parts that are attached to bones and which help us to move

nutrients found in food. Animals and plants need nutrients to stay healthy.

self esteem feeling good about what you can do and how you look

Find out more

Books to read

Look After Yourself: Healthy Food, Angela Royston (Heinemann Library, 2004)

Obesity, Jason Glaser (First Facts Books, 2006)

Why Must I Take Exercise?, Jackie Gaff (Cherrytree Books, 2009)

Websites

http://kidshealth.org/kid/stay_healthy/index.html
This website has tips on healthy eating.

http://www.cyh.com
Click on Kids' Health and follow the links to "Fun and games" to learn more about healthy eating and keeping fit. Or search for "Obesity" to find out more.

http://www.mypyramid.gov/kids/index.html
Visit this link to discover games, tips and activities on eating well and exercise.

Index